Russia's Place in the World in the 21st Century

Robert Skidelsky[1]

About the Author

Professor Lord Robert Skidelsky, Professorial Fellow at the Global Policy Institute at London Metropolitan University, was previously Professor of Political Economy at the University of Warwick. He is the author of *The World After Communism* (1995) and a biography of the economist John Maynard Keynes, which received five prizes, including the Lionel Gelber Prize for International Relations and the Council of Foreign Relations Prize for International Relations. He was elected a Fellow of the British Academy in 1994.

Robert Skidelsky elevated to the House of Lords in 1991 and served as Chief Opposition Spokesman on Treasury Affairs (1998-1999). From 1991 to 2001 he was

Chairman of the Social Market Foundation. Since 2002 he has been Chairman of the Centre for Global Studies.

Lord Skidelsky is a non-executive director of Janus Capital Inc, Chairman of the Greater Europe Fund and a Director of Transnational Insights Ltd. A Russian speaker, he is Director of the Moscow School of Political Studies and Founder and Executive Secretary of The UK/Russia Round Table. He is also a Trustee of the Manhattan Institute and Chairman of the Governors of the Brighton College.

Russia's Place in the World in the 21st Century

Robert Skidelsky[1]

Introduction

The greatest disappointment of the post-Communist era has been the failure of the West's relationship with Russia. Most policy-makers and experts expected that, after an inevitably troublesome period of transition, Russia would join the United States and Europe in a strategic and economic partnership, based on shared interests and values. The pace of change might be doubtful, but not its direction. Today, the area of shared interests has shrunk, and the divergence of values has grown. A resurgent Russia is the world's foremost revionist power, rejecting a *status quo* predicated on the notion of a western victory in the cold war. Its two super-power assets – nuclear weapons and energy – make it a potential leader of all those lesser powers dissatisfied with their present position in the world. A potential Russia-China axis based on shared resistance to US hegemony carries the seeds of a new bipolarity.[2] This essay sets out to explore what Russia's place in the 21st century is likely to be.

Western expectations of post-Communist Russia's trajectory rested on three assumptions. The first was the irreversibility of the loss of empire: 'What has happened has happened, and cannot be reversed (...)'.[3] I shall argue that this view is rejected by most of Russia's elite. The second was the view that the United States would continue to provide the world with 'multilateral' leadership. This view was shattered by the Bush Administration's 'unilateralism': US unilateralism was the cue for Russia to pursue its own. The third was the assumption that Russia would become economically integrated with the west, and especially Europe. This has not yet happened.

It is, of course, difficult to judge how much of the recent upsurge of Russian revisionism is a product of injured pride – a *pis aller* which will yield to the passage of time, globalization, the growth of the middle class, and more tactful handling by the West – and how much of it springs from deep forces in Russian history.

The problem is that history is time-dependent, but never repeats itself exactly. It exhibits a strong cyclical character, but it is not static. In politics and economics, as indeed in science, there is clear evidence of progress, so we must see the cycle more as a spiral. The European Union is a return to the project of multinational empire but in the acceptably democratic form of a multinational union. Russia has similarly experienced a waxing and waning of territory, and the alternating pulls of West and the East. These are permanent forces, but they are unlikely to express themselves in exactly the same way. Furthermore, Russia's ability – as opposed to desire – to change its place in the global pecking order depends on the relations of power in the international system as a whole.

There are two further problems with trying to extrapolate from the past. Though the history of societies exhibits strong continuities, it is punctuated by non-linear moments, techtonic shifts which close some doors, open new ones. Such 'ruptures' are overwhelmingly the result of intrusions from outside the settled state of affairs, whether they be revolutions, wars, economic disasters, or a mixture of all three. But it is in the nature of such moments that we cannot tell what they will be, when they will happen, or what their consequences will be. In Germany, defeat in the first world war produced Hitler; defeat in the second, democracy and pacifism. But it does seem as though major discontinuities are necessary to shift countries onto a new curve, for better or worse. Secondly, it is very hard to fit the present into the past. It simply produces too much 'noise'. We think something is completely new: only in fifty or a hundred years can we see whether it fits into the long *durée*, or whether it is a genuine rupture. All of this is distressingly vague. It is just to caution against ignoring history in thinking about what a 'normal' Russian evolution might be.

The obvious question is: how far has the 'defeat' of 1990-1, which involved large loss of population and territory, overcome the long history of empire and autocracy? To put it differently: how far has it ruptured Russia's 'civilization', which was so bound up with the troubled history of its empire? Has it forced Russia to see itself as a nation rather than as an empire? Has it forced on Russia, willy-nilly, a European rather than a Eurasian future?

New International Doctrine: Multipolarity.

A common interpretation of Russia's contemporary foreign policy is that it lacks an ideological basis.[4] It is true that it has retreated to pragmatism or 'functionalism' in the light of the failures of the ambitious 'partnership' hopes entertained by Gorbachev, Yeltsin, and the early Putin. However, there exists an official doctrine of Russian foreign policy, and, beyond that, the first stirrings of a new ideology of imperialism, which mimics a parallel development in the United States.

'Multipolarity' is the official Russian doctrine of international relations, as it is of China and France. On 28 June 2000, Putin approved a document which read 'Russia shall seek to achieve a multi-polar system of international relations that really reflects the diversity of the modern world'.[5] 'The formation of a multipolar world', wrote Yevgeny Primakov in 2003, 'is the main vector of the world's development'.[6] President Putin echoed him in Munich on 10 February 2007 this year. 'The unipolar world, he said, 'did not take place'. Referring to the rise of the new powers, and especially the so-called BRICs – Brazil, Russia, India, and China, he said, 'There is no reason to doubt that the economic potential of the new centres of global economic growth will inevitably be converted into political influence and will strengthen multipolarity'.[7] The common thread in these pronouncements is Russia's continued view of itself as an 'independent' great power separate from the European Union. As I shall argue, this implies that Russia still sees itself as an empire rather than as a nation-state.

The Russian doctrine of multipolarity is supported by a commonly held interpretation of how the Cold War ended.

How the Cold War Ended: Myth and Reality.

The trauma of post-Soviet Russia has been profound. As Rodric Braithwaite notes: 'After 1991, the Russians lost in short order their ancient empire, their military pride, their political system, their ideology, and their economy'.[8] It was psychologically necessary to construct a narrative which disguised the meaning of this collapse and held out hope of resurrection.

A popular line has been to interpret the events of 1990-1 as a defeat for communism but not for Russia. The Soviet Union was not 'conquered' by the West: it was renounced by the free will of the Russian people. The Baltic Republics were freed by Russia's choice. Russians offered 'a sincere partnership with all the members of the big European family'.[9] Instead, the West trampled all over them, claiming victors' rights, not only over eastern Europe, but over large swathes of former Soviet territory.

Russian conservatives are more ready to acknowledge that the USSR did in fact lose the Cold War. Their argument is that throughout the Cold War the West and the Soviet Union were equals. But the Soviets lost the last round. This was mainly due to Gorbachev.[10] Gorbachev dismantled a 'going concern' and acquiesced in a huge, and unnecessary shift in the balance of power. Yeltsin compounded the defeat by liquidating the Soviet state in order to get rid of Gorbachev, and allowing a rapacious nomenklatura to plunder the Soviet economy. Now Russia has the resources and strong political leadership to 'replay the last round' – to correct the terms on which the Cold War ended. This account gains credibility from the fact that the vast majority of Russians had no inkling in the 1980s that their 'successful' state was about to implode. It is similar to the 'stab in the back' legend which Germans used to explain their defeat in 1918.

A more subtle version of the 'denial of defeat' story has it that in 1991 the United States and the Soviet Union simultaneously ceased to be superpowers. Each had created global coalitions to contain the other. Once this need disappeared, America's command over its allies disappeared just as surely as did the Soviet command over its world – hence the emergence of multipolarity.[11] The fact that the coalition of western states led by America was vastly more powerful, wealthy, and legitimate than the coalition Moscow assembled against it is conveniently ignored.

By contrast, narratives of Russian liberals, which accept both the end of communism and the end of

Russian empire as good things, and actively seek integration with the West, have almost no domestic resonance. Partly this is because they are associated with the chaos and economic meltdown of the Yeltsin years; also because they are are associated with western encroachments on the Russian space. Had the policies of Yeltsin not been identified with the 'theft' of the Russian patrimony by oligarchs and western interests, liberal narratives would have had more success.

There is some truth in the Russian interpretations. Like the British empire, the Soviet empire was voluntarily liquidated. But of course, the language of voluntarism masks a huge defeat for the Soviet world. As Dominic Lieven notes: 'In the absence of all-out military conflict, the West was always likely to win the Cold War. American resources were much greater than those of the Soviet Union. Its economic power in particular was an enormous asset in winning allies, wooing clients and providing a vision of the 'good life' which had mass appeal'.[12] The moment of truth came in 1983, and particularly following the announcement of 'Star Wars', with the realization by the Russian leadership that the United States had both the capacity and the will to outbuild the Soviet Union. Their illusion was the belief that Russia was in a position to make symmetrical arms control agreements with the United States, without being required to make asymmetrical political concessions.

The belief that the collapse of the Soviet Union involved some sort of betrayal, whether by the west or by Gorbachev and Yeltsin, is congruent with one of the most important lessons Russians are apt to draw from their history. This is that no defeat is final. Over 500 years the Russian empire has advanced and retreated, but after each setback has been able to recover territory and resume its expansion. Russians remember the 'time of troubles at the start of the 17th century when the Russian state almost ceased to exist: an experience repeated in the 1990s. They remember Prince Gorchakov's success in reversing the Treaty of Paris which followed Russia's defeat in the Crimean War. They remember that the Treaty of Brest-Litovsk in 1918 pushed Russia's western borders back to where they had been before Peter the Great, but that within a few years the Soviets had restored most of them, and that after 1945 were able to push their empire into central Europe. Today Russia's European frontiers are back to where they were in 1918 (that is 1700) and they have also surrendered five republics in Central Asia. Their own history provides no compelling argument for them to accept these losses as permanent.

There is an instructive contrast to be drawn with the end of the European colonial empires. The British and French empires were overseas empires, whose shedding did not impinge on the integrity of the nation, whereas the Soviet Union, like its Tsarist predecessor, was a continental empire, lacking natural frontiers, in which the distinction between nation and empire was always fuzzy.[13] Their empire, that is, was part of the Russian 'identity' in a way that their overseas empires never were for the British and French. It was also a central component of Russian power. It is as difficult for Russia to accept the permanent loss of the Ukraine as it would be for the United States to accept the secession of, say, Massachusetts.

A New Ideology of Empire

Russian thoughts about how to retrieve their global position turn naturally to the need to recover a high degree of control over the Soviet space surrendered by Yeltsin in 1991. This is mainly disguised, but the imperial hoof-beat is starting to be heard. What I call Russia's 'imperial project' is precisely this: restoring Moscow's rule, direct or indirect, wholly or in part, over territories that were part of the Soviet Union, and before that, of the Tsarist empire. It is not official policy. The vote of the Russian Duma annulling the dissolution of the USSR in 1996 was purely symbolic. But there are now two more substantial ideologies of recovery: Anatoly Chubais's doctrine of 'liberal empire' and Vladislav Surkov's doctrine of 'sovereign democracy'. Chubais, architect of Yeltsin's victory in 1996, is head of the electricity monopoly, UES; Surkov is deputy head of Putin's Presidential Administration, and heads 'the Kremlin's political science laboratory'.[14]

Chubais's theory of 'liberal empire' was first aired in September 2003. Mixing hyperbole with regret, he claimed that in 1991 'the greatest empire of all time ceased to exist'. Russia should now construct a 'liberal empire' from the pieces of the old Soviet Union. While respecting its neighbours 'inviolability of borders and territorial integrity', Russia's 'mission' should be to promote Russian culture and protect the Russian populations in its 'neighbourhood', establish a dominant position in its neighbours' trade and business ('in the acquisition and development of assets') and guarantee their 'freedom and democracy'. 'It's high time to call a spade a spade' Chubais said. Russia was the 'natural and unique leader' of the Confederation of Independent States. Its strategic task was to 'beef up, increase and strengthen its leadership position in this part of the globe'. Only thus, Chubais argued, 'can Russia occupy its natural place alongside the United States, the European Union and Japan, in a ring of great democracies… the place designated for it by history'.[15]

Chubais's language of liberal empire mimics post-Iraq discussion of America's role in the world, as in Niall Ferguson case for American ' liberal empire' in his book *Colossus* (2004).[16] However, the willingness of a Russian leader to use imperial language reflects the fact that Russians feel much less guilty than do western elites about their imperial past, mainly because most Russians thought of the Tsarist empire, and then the Soviet Union, as an extension of their own nation, not as conquered territory.

Surkov's phrase 'sovereign democracy' dates from a speech to a United Russia seminar in February 2006. He means by it the right of Russians to make their own decisions. This requires a strong government in a continental-sized state, able to use its energy windfalls to diversify the Russian economy, make it respected in the world, and reverse the incentive of the Russian elite to become an 'offshore aristocracy'. For Surkov, as for most Russians, Russia was 'on the verge of losing its sovereignty' under Yeltsin. Political break-up and economic liberalisation led to extraordinary accumulations of private plunder. Without democracy Russia will be unstable. But without sovereignty, foreign powers will use its democracy to undermine Russian independence. Russia can protect its sovereignty by re-establishing its dominance over its near abroad. 'For 500 years [Russia] was a modern state. It made history and was not made by it', Surkov says, 'We differ strongly' from Slovaks, Baltic nations and even Ukrainians – they had no state system... Russian politicians of the past drew them on maps'.[17]

The statements of Chubais and Surkov must be contrasted with more traditional calls, like that of Solzhenitsyn, for a re-centering of a Slavic core, which draws on the late tsarist legacies of slavophilism and Orthodoxy. Russia, Belorussia, and Ukraine were all part of the Kievan Rus. Seventy-nine per cent of Russians believe that Russians, Ukrainians and Belorussians are three branches of a single Slavic nation; 70 per cent of Russians do not perceive Ukraine as a foreign state.[18] Although happy enough to draw on such sentiment, Chubais and Surkov claim to be modernist and pragmatic in their approach. The question they address is: what are the conditions of independence in today's world? How is independence to be preserved against the triple challenge of American domination, globalization, and ethnic nationalism?

Their answer lies in the multipolar organization of states, but it is evident that only some states can be sovereign. A hierarchy of states is a fact of life. Some countries are fated to be sovereign, others to be subjects; some to be spiders others to be flies. Russia is one of the world's natural sovereigns, made so by its size, its resources, its political will. Backing this approach is the view that small nation-states are doomed by globalization. They are too weak to defend their sovereignty, politically, strategically, or economically. The alternative they face is either to be gobbled up by the American 'world empire' or to join great powers in new forms of 'collective imperial sovereignty'. Russians see themselves caught in America's spider web: they demand the right to weave one of their own. Their neo-imperialism is a matter-of-fact solution to the problem, as they see it, of a unipolar world in an age when the idea of territorial imperialism is bankrupt.

The new ideology of empire is underpinned by three arguments: the 'logic' of geopolitics, rejection by the West, and the potential to exploit Russia's newly-acquired position as an energy superpower.

Geopolitics

The influence of geopolitics stems from Russia's position astride Europe and Asia. This makes it feel both superior and vulnerable. Its immense size and reach make it the neighbour that no country can afford to ignore. Policy makers in Europe, the Middle East, Central Asia and the Far East must all take Russia into account. It may not be a world power like the USA, but it remains a continental-sized one with its fingers in everyone else's pies. On the other hand, Russia's immense spread leaves it vulnerable to attack on many frontiers, a weakness confirmed by its historical experience of invasions. To be secure it feels it needs to control much more of the Eurasian heartland than it currently does. It has felt keenly the loss of the geographical buffers that enabled it three times to organise a successful defence in depth against a western invader.[19] Now the potential enemy – the United States, NATO – is encamped much closer to Russia's heart. The fear of military invasion may seem fanciful today, but the fear, for instance, of the west using Muslim states to confine Russia is long-standing, and is reinforced by the US presence in the Caucasus and central Asia.[20] There is also a fear of economic strangulation. Lieven notes that 'any state as dependent for its prosperity on rivers as was the case with early modern Russia was almost certain to seek control of the whole extent of these rivers and their exits to the sea. To do otherwise was to allow foreign and, very probably, hostile states to tax and interdict one's trade at will'.[21] Today's reflex is the demand to control the pipelines which carry Russian oil and gas through the country and abroad. This means control of the territories through which the pipes run.

'The West does not Love Us'
This perception is near ubiquitous, and long-standing. The West repudiated Russia's overtures, so it must carve out for itself a separate destiny. Chubais says: 'We must not join the EU or NATO. We do not 'fit' there either economically, politically or geographically.'[22] Surkov echoes him: 'It would be good to flee to Europe, but they will not receive us there...It is better to be enemies and not ambiguous friends as is the case now!'[23] Rejection of a subordinate European future could not be clearer.

The love-hate relationship with the West has, of course,

been a *leitmotiv* of Russian history. As the wife of Tsar Paul I remarked to the French visitor Custine in 1839: 'If you think well of us, you will say so, but it will be useless; you will not be believed: we are ill-understood, and people will not understand us better'.[24] The urgent desire to catch up the West; imitation followed by a sense of rejection; the turning back to a non-Western vision of Russia, whether Eurasian, Orthodox, or just simply Russian; the inability to find a balance between what Russia needs to share with the West to be modern, and what it needs to retain to stay Russian: all these themes have been played out repeatedly. As Lieven points out, Eurasianism was a spin-off of Russia's sense of inferiority to, and rejection by, the West. He quotes Dostoyevsky: 'In Europe we were hangers-on and slaves, whereas in Asia we shall go as masters'.[25]

In Griboyedev's play, *'Tis Folly to be Wise*, Chatsky talks about a Frenchman who set out from Paris to educate the barbaric Russians and on his arrival in Russia, met 'no Russian faces, no Russian sounds', just lots of Russians pretending to be French. This led him to a famous outburst: let God 'exorcise this unclean spirit of hollow slavish mindless imitation', and rescue 'our customs, language and the good old days' from 'our sickening love of foreign ways'. The trouble was that 'foreign ways' were the means to great power status. This tension between the imperatives of economic modernization and the maintenance of the autocracy ran through tsarist Russia. It was apparently overcome under communism by adopting a non-western model of economic development. It has resurfaced in Putin's attempt to balance the *siloviki* and economic reformers in his government.

Putin started as a sincere Europeanist. There was a ready-made axis – following on from the Ostpolitik of the 1970s – between Russia and Germany, and Putin's own time as a KGB officer in Germany. Putin had a notably warm relationship with former Chancellor Gerhard Schroeder, and vestiges of it remain with Schroeder's successor Angela Merkel. Germany has backed the Baltic gas pipeline, against the wishes of Poland and the Baltic states. Russia joined France and Germany in opposing the Iraq war. President Chirac hoped that this would grow into a permanent counter-balance to US hegemony. But for his successor, Nicolas Sarkozy, the priority is to restore France's position within the EU and improve relations with the United States.

EU enlargement has shattered the idea of a 'natural' EU-Russian partnership, by making members of vociferously anti-Russian states like Poland and Estonia.[26] The chief priority of the former Soviet satellites is to use the EU and NATO to contain Russia, whereas Russia's desire was for a partnership with Europe to contain the United States. As Russia's hopes for partnership with the EU faded, it has started to treat the entity with ill-disguised contempt, preferring to 'divide and rule' through bilateral arrangements with the powerful members. There is now active rivalry between the EU and Russia for control of the 'post-Soviet space'. Russia is not part of the EU's 'Neighbourhood Policy'.The four 'comon spaces' of cooperation (economics and trade; internal security; foreign and security policy;

education, science, and culture) have barely moved beyond the discussion stage. Poland has blocked talks to replace the almost moribund Partnership and Cooperation Agreement, set to expire in November 2007, because Russia bans Polish meat from its market. There is no agreement on energy security. Russia opposes the EU's plans for Kosovo. The bi-annual EU-Russia summits have become increasingly bad-tempered.[27]

All this was fairly predictable in light of the shift of Russia's frontier eastwards: Russia has ceased to matter so much in the European balance of power system. But, in addition, Putin's policy of making Russia an integral part of 'the concert of European nations' was inconsistent with his determination to keep 'Russian internal policy... exclusively a Russian concern'.[28] If the EU stands for anything it is democracy, human rights, civil liberties, and Russia's internal politics have affronted all three. Today Russia is less part of the political structure of Europe than it was before the first world war, or even in Soviet times.

The economic relationship between Russia and EU while quantitatively impressive (over 50 per cent of Russia's trade is with the EU) is very narrowly based. Russia's trade with the EU consists mainly of an exchange of commodities for machinery and consumer goods. Trade in services is small in comparison and one-sided: Russia buys financial services and sends tourists. The picture is one of pragmatic cooperation but very little integration. Russia still sees its economic relationship with the EU – and indeed with most other countries – in terms of deals between para-statal companies, rather than market integration: a relic of old Soviet thinking which still impedes Russia's accession to the World Trade Organization. At the official level, 'the goal of incremental integration has given way to the goal of pragmatic coexistence between separate entities European and Russo-Eurasian'.[29]

Putin's relationship with US has failed too, despite his warm feelings towards President Bush. He invested a lot of political capital in it in the first couple of years of his presidency. He brilliantly exploited the opportunity opened up by 9/11 to construct an anti-terrorist coalition. He was the first to telephone Bush after the terrorist attack on New York and the Pentagon. Overruling his military, he gave unconditional support to the US in Afghanistan, and military access to central Asian countries bound to Russia by security treaty, while closing down Russian bases in Cuba and Vietnam. He acceded to the American request to lower the price of oil. He was ready to discard earlier Russian insistence on the primacy of Security Council resolutions, and hinted that the US anti-missile shield programme could be developed in the context of the ABM Treaty.[30] Officials from both sides started to talk about a 'strategic partnership'. The Russian elite started to compare the anti-terrorist coalition with the anti-Hitler alliance, and fondly recalled FDR's 'big policemen' model of postwar arrangements.

But the pay-off was meagre. There was satisfactory silence on Chechnya, but Russia was not offered a fast track to WTO membership, or a meaningful security role in NATO and the Middle East. Putin had hoped to get

NATO involved in Russia's military reforms.[31] Instead NATO frontline troops were established on the soil of its neighbours, and NATO has started on the process of admitting all nine former Warsaw Pact members, while shelving plans to include Russia as a partner.[32] America unilaterally abrogated the ABM treaty, thus precipitating the collapse of the arms control regime. Moreover, a series of US-inspired (or at least CIA-financed) 'coloured' revolutions in Serbia, Georgia and Ukraine have increased Russia's sense of isolation and paranoia by depriving it of reliable clients. Russia retaliated by joining France and Germany in opposing the Iraq war; and has been out of step with the west on Kosovo and Iran. Dmitri Trenin, director of the liberal Carnegie Moscow Centre, had looked forward to a 'quasi-alliance' with the United States in 2001. By 2006 he was lamenting 'the decoupling of Russia from the West'.[33] At Munich, on 10 February 2007, Putin sounded like a jilted lover. He still thought of President George W. Bush as his friend, but realized that 'the system of international relations is just like mathematics. There are no personal dimensions'.

To put it in a nutshell, Putin's geopolitical strategy lies in ruins. Failing to grasp the extent of the demands the EU would make of it or the irrelevance to the United States of Moscow's loyalty, the Kremlin has retreated to purely 'functional relationships'. This is the seed from which the 'imperial project' sprouts.

Energy Superpower
The material basis of current Russian self-assertiveness is the dramatic improvement in its economic position: a

full treasury, freedom from foreign loans, above all its emergence as an 'energy superpower'.

The phrase needs explanation. As late as 1999, the *Economist* looked forward to 'a world in which supply and demand [in energy] were determined not by geopolitics and cartels, but by geology and markets', musing that this state of affairs would force down the price of oil to $5 a barrel.[34] In a competitive market, the producer of energy has no power: energy cannot be used for foreign policy or for any purpose other than to supply consumers at prices they are willing to pay, to the mutual benefit of both. But this is not the world in which we live.The fact that there are only a few major sources of supply for a commodity which is in high and growing demand, and for which there is no ready substitute, gives the producers of that commodity market power. In energy, producer cartels and oligopolies dominate the market. Such producer organizations can fix prices. But if, in addition, producer groups are under political control, governments can use this control for foreign policy purposes. Ever since OPEC quadrupled oil prices and interdicted supply during the Arab-Israeli war of 1973-4 the world has worried about 'energy security'.

Russia is well placed to exploit both the 'economic' and the 'geopolitical' potential of energy. It has the world's largest reserves of natural gas and is the world's second largest exporter of oil after Saudi Arabia. Putin has made the oil and gas sectors his power base, domestically and internationally. In 1994, the Kremlin wrested control of oil from the oil barons by dismantling the largest private producer Yukos, and has boosted the monopoly position of Gazprom, the state gas company, as part of its policy of keeping 'strategic sectors' of the economy under national control. State control of these resources boosts sovereignty in the precise sense defined by Surkov: that is, by boosting independence. It makes you less dependent on others than others are on you. CIS countries are almost totally dependent on Russian supplies of energy and/or Russian-owned pipelines. Russia has also begun acquiring ownership of oil and gas assets in its former Central Asian republics, especially in Kazakhstan.[35] The EU is dependent on Gazprom for one-quarter of its energy needs.

This puts Russia in a position to use energy as an instrument of imperial restoration in the former Soviet space, and to bargain with the EU about 'energy security'. It aims to buy the political loyalty of the western CIS republics in return for cheap energy; but is ready to punish them by interrupting supply if they veer too closely to the west. The EU's vulnerability to interrupted supply was brought home when Russia temporarily stopped natural gas deliveries to the Ukraine on 1 January 2006, which had a knock-on effect on gas deliveries from the Ukraine to Europe. The same year, Gazprom signed a Baltic pipeline deal with the German BASG and Eon to supply gas directly to Germany, by-passing Poland and other east European countries. Although Russia claims to be a 'reliable supplier', its actions suggest the contrary. Gazprom has threatened to withhold supply unless it was allowed to invest in downstream business in the EU. Its proposal to build a pipeline to China from western Siberia which is the main source of gas to Europe suggests that future supply will be subject to arbitrage between Europe and China. This will create an artificial shortage, pushing up prices. In response to Russia's 'oil and gas imperialism',[36] the EU Commission has tried to build a counter-cartel of oil-consuming nations to bargain with Russia. The Commission aims to force the complete separation of energy networks from companies that supply gas and electricity. The deal would allow Gazprom to acquire downstream facilities in the EU on condition that it offered EU companies reciprocal facilities to buy its own pipelines.[37]

Part of the EU's worry is not that Russia might turn the taps off, but that it might fail to increase its capacity to meet Europe's growing demand. The EU's response has been to encourage Russia to open its energy market to foreign investment. Russia's incentives are different. Its Stabilization Fund has built up a huge surplus, so it does not need to sell more oil and gas. Russians also point out that the US can print as many dollars as it wants to enable other countries to buy Russia's energy. But energy is a non-renewable resource, which needs to be preserved, not squandered.

The doctrines of 'liberal empire' and 'sovereign democracy' are designed to provide an ideological underpinning for the attempt to reconstitute, in modern clothes, the Tsarist empire and its Soviet successor, as a condition for a new global balance of great powers. This is the Russian project. But what is desired is not the same as what is possible. The latter depends on 'objective facts', including the response of others to Russian actions. In the concluding part of this essay I want to consider the possibilities of realizing the two connected parts of the 'grand design'.

Reconstitution of the Empire

The Soviet Union collapsed, in part, because it failed 'to square the demands of power, which required a state of continental size, with the challenge presented by ethnic nationalism'.[38] The doctrines of 'liberal empire' and 'sovereign democracy' recapitulate this dilemma, but add to it the real danger of conflict with the west. Twenty-five million ethnic Russians and a further 100 million non-Russian subjects were 'lost' to the empire when the Soviet Union collapsed. Russia's claim to be the protector of the rights and interests of all Russians in the former Soviet Union is a claim to a right of intervention. This is not only incompatible with the promise to respect its neighbours' borders, but risks a miliary confrontation with the West in states like Latvia and Estonia, which have large Russian minorities and whose independence is guaranteed by the EU and NATO. Further potential for conflict arises from Putin's implicit threat to dislodge the US from its positions in the Caucasus and Central Asia and his military doctrine that defines the frontiers of the former Soviet republics as the strategic frontiers of the Russian Federation.[39]

Chubais has shifted the emphasis of 'liberal empire' from the potentially explosive issues of frontiers and Russian *irridenta* to energy and business links. In its more modest version it boils down to manipulating the internal politics and economics of the CIS states so as to keep them within Russia's 'sphere of influence'.

However, there are big difficulties in the way of Moscow creating client states through political and business manipulation. Most post-Communist leaders in Europe and the Caucasus (Lukashenko of Belarus is a notorious exception) have created their political identity by positioning themselves as independent, pro-Western democrats. This is particularly true in the Ukraine and Georgia. This means that Russian-backed candidates do not always win elections. Imperial activism on its western borders has been marked by series of defeats, the most painful being Russia's failed interference in Ukrainian elections of 2004. Nor could Russia affect election results in Moldova. Its hold over Georgia was upset by the collapse of the Sheverdnadze regime in November 2003, and it had to promise to withdraw its troops. As a result of such reverses, Russia is tempted to exploit 'frozen conflicts' in Abkhazia, South Ossetia, Nagorno-Karabakh, and Transdnestria to destabilize the Caucasus and Moldova. But this may be a losing game, since leaders like Sakaashvili can use these conflicts to lever support from the West. Putin's centralizing drive within the Russian Federation – which includes the war to prevent Chechnyan independence – undermines any belief by states currently detached from Russia that Russia will champion their autonomy in an expanded Russian federation: there is unlikely to be a Russian equivalent of Hong Kong. Even Belarus is unenthusiastic about joining a Greater Russia.[40] Arkady Moshes argues that Georgia, Moldova, Belarus and Ukraine constitute an emergent identity 'Intermediate Europe', not ready for integration into EU-Atlantic structures, but increasingly de-coupled from Russia.[41]

On the economic side, Russia can threaten energy and trade sanctions, but these are double-edged weapons. Cutting energy supplies to Ukraine and Belarus jeopardises energy exports to the EU, and in any case energy subsidies are being phased out. Closing labour markets to CIS migrants damages the construction and services industries. Slapping on trade embargoes goes against the interests of Russian business expansion.

Nor does Russia offer its former republics a model of success. It does not lead in economic growth, it is riddled with crime and corruption. In GDP at PPP per capita Russia ranks 59th in the world with $12,178, well under half the EU average.[42] The UN Human Development Index (which takes account of life expectancy and education) puts Russia in 65th place, roughly the same as Brazil, with Poland far ahead at 37.[43] The Council of Europe has kept up a barrage on Russia's record on human rights.

Finally, imperialism today lacks a doctrinal basis. Tsarism offered dynastic loyalty, Pan-Slavism, Orthodoxy. The Soviet Union had communism. Today's Russian imperialists are forced to be pragmatists. In a world where success is increasingly measured by economic prosperity and human security, the EU, the US, and even China offer alternative poles of attraction, even for Russians. The world economy would have to go horribly wrong for ancient tribal loyalties to determine Russia's future.

Given the failure of liberal empire in the west, it is not surprising that Russia has recently switched emphasis reintegrating the five newly independent, but landlocked, countries of Central Asia, where its exports of capital and autocracy are more welcome. Russia backed Uzbekistan in the face of criticism from the US and the EU over its brutal suppression of a rebellion in Andijan on 13 May 2005. In return, Karimov severed ties with America and, five months later, signed the 'Treaty on Allied Relations' granting Russia the right to use military force on Uzbek territory.[44] This follows security agreements already in place with Tajikstan, Kazakhstan and Kyrgyzstan. Russia's rapprochement with its Central Asian neighbours also has important commercial dimensions. Both agreements with Tajikistan and Uzbekistan gave Russian companies priority in large-scale projects and privatizations, and with both countries desperate for foreign investment Russia looks set to buy liberal empire with its petrodollars. Keeping the region's corrupt dictators afloat also offers Russia a bulwark against the spread of radical Islam from unstable countries to the South.

However, this is not the end of the story. It is quite conceivable that Russia's 'soft power' – the power of attraction – will grow organically from the seeds already there: the Russian language, still the *lingua franca* throughout the CIS, the Russian *irridenta* scattered through the 'near abroad', and Russian culture, increasingly accessible through satellite TV channels and Russian films. Russia could do much more than it currently does to encourage tourism, for example by introducing 'unilateral visa disarmament'.[45] This would open its borders to EU nationals, including those from

Eastern European states. A single bold action like this could have an immediate impact on how Russia is perceived in the West and its near abroad. Although it is claimed that Russia cannot provide CIS countries with 'an attractive model of socio-economic and political development', it is also true that migration into Russia 'has become Eurasia's safety valve'.[46]

But the main missing ingredient in Russia's 'soft power' is the perception of success. The more successful Russia is seen to be as an economy, a polity, and a society the more attractive it will become to Russians and others living beyond its borders.

The Challenge to the United States

Russia rejects America's right to rule the world; it denies that it has the power to do so. These are different claims, the first affecting legitimacy, the second capability. In the recent international relations literature the distinction has become blurred, because of acceptance of 'soft power'as a key component of capability. The question is: will America have enough power – in this enlarged sense – to remain the world's only 'superpower' for the foreseeable future?

Polarity is about the distribution of power within the international system. Multi-polarity describes a distribution of power in which more than two states have nearly equal amounts of military, cultural and economic influence. On the surface multi-polarity seems far away. In relative terms, the United States 'is militarily more powerful than any political entity since the Roman Empire'.[47] It is the world's largest economy, by far the world's largest defence spender, and the only country which continually upgrades its military technology. Deepak Lal calculates that 'based on past and current [economic] performance and future prospects, the only potential competitors to US military power are the Chinese (by perhaps mid-century) and the Indians by the end of the century'. But 'given the US technological lead, these potential dates for military catch-up are likely to be even later'. Thus he is able to conclude that 'for at least this century it is unlikely that US military power will be challenged'.[48] But America's technological lead may not mean as much as is claimed for it. Iraq shows that 'asymmetric warfare' can partly neutralize it. Terrorist actions do not require much in the way of resources or technology. Edward Luttwak has argued that the US does not possess enough ruthlessness to win wars against terrorists.[49]

A somewhat different perspective is given by the 'Correlates of War' project of the University of Michigan. This aims to measure the distribution of power in the international system as a whole. To this end it has calculated an index of the 'coefficient of power' in the world since 1816, where zero represents perfect equality and one perfect concentration. Its main long-run finding is that power tends to concentrate during and immediately after big wars and then to disperse, 'Global system concentration' (counting only the half dozen great powers) has steadily declined from 0.4 per cent in 1946 to 0.22 in 2001. In 1946, the United States had just over 50 per cent of great power military capability, the Soviet Union was second with 20 per cent, and Britain third with 10 per cent. By 2001, the United States had 30 per cent, Russia had shrunk to 12 per cent, China had come up to 20 per cent. (China's high score reflects population and size of economy in the weighting).[50] So although the 'hard power' asymmetry is still there, it is much less marked than it was in 1945. Such calculations need to be taken with a large pinch of salt, but one can see that the makings of a global balance of power system of a 'mathematical' kind do exist, on the basis of alliances of the weaker great powers to check the stronger.

However, the 'Correlates of War' methodology may still overestimate US capabilities. Not size of economies but size of manufacturing base should be compared. The size of the manufacturing sector in the US economy has shrunk from 37 per cent in 1960 to 18 per cent today.[51] On present free trade policy the United States is set to lose practically all its manufacturing industry in a decade or two.

The Russian thesis of an evolution towards multi-polarity is thus perfectly plausible. A separate question is whether Russia will be one of the 'poles'. Most Russian elites think it inconceivable that it will not be. But this is not obvious. Three of the 'correlates' of power considered by the Michigan project are population, size of economy, and political system, the last two relevant to the ability to mobilise hard power and project 'soft power' respectively. Russia's performance in all three areas raise doubts about its future as a global power.

Demography
For Russia this is a well-known disaster area. The population of the USSR was 293 million in 1990, the

USA's 255 million. In 1993 the population of Russian Federation was 149m. So Russia lost about 140 million people when the Soviet Union broke up. This loss has been compounded by the subseqent decline of the Russian population as a result of an increase in the death rate and simultaneous decrease in birth rate. It is projected to fall from 143 million today to between 137 million and 125 million in 20 years time, and down to below100 million by 2050.[52] America's population has meanwhile risen to 300 million, and is expected to stay there. These figures are of course, dwarfed by China and India. Male life expectancy in Russia has fallen to below 60, largely due to alcoholism, suicide, industrial accidents, murders, etc... Russian women live longer but they too lag up to 10 years behind their western counterparts. The quality of Russia's population may also be falling as educated Russians flock abroad, to be replaced by low-paid manual workers. One expert has written that 'no other country has such a negative combination of demographic indicators as Russia, even among the least developed countries in the world'.[53] Dmitry Gorenberg argues that Russia's demographic decline has been exaggerated. 'While Russia's population is not likely to grow in the coming years, it is likely to shrink far less rapidly than previous estimates predicted' he writes.[54] But this is a modification of an accepted trend.

Russia's problem is not only the size of its population but also its distribution. The Soviets settled 30m Russians east of the Urals, but many are now trickling back to European Russia. Today only 18 million Russians live in the far east.[55] Everyone (Russians and migrants) wants to live in large cities in the western part of Russia, and no one wants to live in the east. So there are not enough Russians to settle and defend most of their country – at least by conventional means.

It is generally agreed that the negative economic and political consequences of a declining population can only be offset through migration. But Russian nationalism is hostile to the immigration of non-Slavs like Armenians, Caucasians, and Asians. Two hundred thousand Chinese live in Russia, mostly across from the Manchurian border, but the Chinese are portrayed as wanting to annex their underpopulated eastern territories. Figures are cited showing that the percentage of ethnic Russians in the Russian Federation has fallen from 80 per cent in 1989 to 70 per cent today. At present immigration policy concentrates on encouraging Russian migrants from former Soviet republics, of whom there is a pool of some 25m.

Demographic trends face Russia with a choice between two futures: that of nation or multinational empire. Russia could aim to consolidate ethnic Russians within a shrunken European and central Asian 'space', with a possible future within, rather than apart from, the European Union. Or, like the Tsars and the Soviets, Russia could adopt a conscious state policy to develop eastern Russia. Companies like Gazprom and Rosneft could increase their investments into oil and gas exploration in eastern Siberia,where most of potential oil and gas is located.[56] But any policy of developing eastern Siberia requires drastic revision of current attitudes to foreign investment in the energy sector and immigration from Asia. Liberal empire means multinationalism, or it is an empty phrase.

Economy

The United States is the largest economy in the world with a GDP at PPP of $ 13 trillion dollars, followed by China with $10.1 trillion. Russia is 9th with $1.7 trillion, about the size of Italy and Brazil.[57]

Energy is predominant both in Russia's domestic economy and foreign trade. Since 2000 there has been a close correlation between GDP growth and the growth of oil export revenues, as the price of Urals oil rose from below $10 to above $70 and more a barrel. In 2005, after six years of economic growth averaging just under 7 per cent a year, oil and gas made up 20 per cent of GDP, more than 60 percent of exports, and 40 percent of budget revenues (some say it is 60-80 percent if related industries are taken into account).[58] The dominance of the energy economy is the direct result of the failed Soviet industrialization. Soviet-style development was dictated not by comparative advantage, but by military imperatives. Most Russian products could not be sold on world markets. Despite high levels of scientific and technical manpower, this lack of marketeability forced the post-Soviet economy back on its natural resource base. The Tsarist economy depended on grain and timber exports. The present equivalent is energy exports. Today Russia is more dependent on its natural resources than in Soviet times, a unique type of de-industrialization.

Russia has started to diversify its economy. This is only prudent, as a large fall in the price of oil can wreck the budget, and put economic growth into reverse.[59] But there is an issue about how far diversification should be pressed, which is bound up with the political debate about Russia's future. The Westernizers (or Europeanists) favour integration into the European economy as a basis for political partnership. The Eurasians are attracted by the idea of using energy to maintain Russia as an independent power centre, balancing between Europe and Asia.The dynamism of China has encouraged talk of creating an East Asian hydrocarbon market on the basis of Russian energy resources. The Eurasianists are currently winning the argument, because the energy economy has structural features which tends towards its self-perpetuation. These go under the collective title of the 'natural resource' curse.

The most familiar of these is the so-called 'Dutch disease', in which cash inflows from energy exports weaken the competitiveness of non-energy sectors by strengthening the currency. This has already started to happen. An appreciating ruble has weakened exports and boosted imports. The tradable sectors of GDP are growing below average, so the huge current account surplus is contracting. The long-run impact of the 'curse' is felt on domestic policy and politics. Four such impacts can be identified.

First, natural resources are viewed as part of the nation's inheritance that have to be kept under state control. This divides the Russian economy into a 'strategic sector' controlled by the Kremlin, and a private enterprise sector outside it. The strategic sector (undefined) exhibits a neo-patrimonial form of political economy in which power and wealth are fused together.

Far from liberalizing its energy markets, the Kremlin has consolidated Gazprom's monopoly and has progressively brought oil production under state control. Its policy of keeping property rights fluid in order to allow for further consolidation under state control deters both domestic and foreign investment in the energy economy.[60] The neo-patrimonial economy also creates a huge problem for the political succession, since the transfer of power always involves the redistribution of property.

Secondly, natural resource abundance diverts economic energy from creating wealth into distributing it. Russian economic life is dominated by the struggle for rents – at all levels of the economy. These rents are shared between the government (in revenues and bribes), the owners of oil and gas companies, and the consumers (in the form of subsidized prices). The real issue at the heart of the Yukos affair was the redistribution of Russia's oil assets and windfall profits.[61] Thirdly, a natural resource-based economy encourages autocracy by giving the government a revenue base outside the income tax system, and thus less need for popular support for its policies. An independent revenue base sustained the autocracy throughout Russian history: first land, then oil. Today the share of government revenues from energy would have reached 100 per cent had not the Stabilization Fund been created. The Russian economist Sergei Guriev has found that a free media is less likely to emerge in resource rich economies, and that this results in a lower rate of growth.[62] Finally, natural resource abundance leads to a struggle for control of territory. The uneven distribution of resources encourages resource-rich regions to break away or encourages resource-poor regions to establish control over the whole country by authoritarian means. Autocracy and centralization, the great continuities in Russia's political system, are thus firmly rooted in Russia's resource geography.[63] They are also self-perpetuating. Their geopolitical implications dominate Russian thinking about how to secure its 'space' and conduct its foreign policy.

In principle, there is no reason why the energy economy should not continue to grow in absolute terms, but decline as a proportion of Russian GDP. However, concentration on the political use of energy may prevent this benign economic development. In the short-run energy allows Russia to cut a striking figure on the world stage. In the long-run it may, by failing to provide enough economic activity for its scientists and engineers, prevent it from realizing its economic potential.

Political System
Russia's place in the international club of great powers depends on its ability to develop a more 'western' political system. Democracy can take many forms, but its core principle, of accountability of governments to voters, is an important source of power, at home and abroad. Autocracy is weak domestically and unattractive externally. At home, it alienates the state from the masses, restricting its ability to mobilise support. Putin's inability to reform the military is a telling index of its limitation: personal popularity is no substitute for a 'democratic mandate'. Autocracy provides no incentive – except possibly in Central Asia – for the reintegration

of the CIS into Chubais's 'liberal empire', and it makes Russia a problematic member for the 'democratic clubs' which it wishes to join.

Russia has experienced liberalising episodes 'from above' before – with Speransky under Tsar Alexander I, with the Duma after 1905. In both cases, autocracy reasserted itself. The big question is: do the tentative steps towards democracy which developed under Gorbachev and Yeltsin represent a decisive rupture with the tradition of autocracy or are they simply temporary deviations from a persisting tendency for autocratic government? Has Russia's political 'genetic code' remained more or less intact?

Richard Pipes is the best known exponent of the continuity thesis. Russia's incapacity for freedom is rooted in the long history of the 'patrimonial state'.[64] Recent evidence from opinion polls reveal 'a preference for order over freedom, suspicion of democracy and the free market, and nostalgia for the Soviet Union'.[65] Against this it can be argued that the current turning away from democracy is not the consequence of ancient history but an understandable response to the weakness and corruption of government in the post-communist period. The restoration of the state and the economy, the humbling of the oligarchs, the curtailment of corruption and gangsterism, were bound to be top priorities for any post-Yeltsin government.[66] Yet the accelerating momentum to centralise and control, beyond any reasonable requirements for a strong state or the 'war on terrorism', does suggest that a historical reflex may be at work.

The continuity theorists can point to the absence in the Russian political tradition of any doctrine of restraint on the ruler's actions. For almost 500 years 'The Russian tsar's power was unconstrained by a constitution, by laws or by representative institutions'.[67] Lacking real feudalism, or a dense network of self-governing towns, Russia's political tradition is more akin to Oriental despotism. It is indisputably part of Christendom, but since Byzantium, Russian Orthodoxy has been a form of Caesaropapism, more like Islam than Protestantism or even Catholicism. As Berdyaev put it, 'In Russia God's things are rendered to Caesar'. A corollary is political messianism – all are equal before the God/Tsar – which is the specifically Russian root of communism.

There is no internal escape, therefore, from the tradition of absolute monarchy. Whether, as Martin Malia believes, the fragile Russian liberalism of the silver age would have broken the hold of despotism but for the first world war remains the great unanswered question. Instead Lenin's Bolshevik state was built on the foundations of Tsarist autocracy. With the exception of Catherine, the great Russian rulers have been the most terrible ones: Ivan IV, Peter the Great, Stalin.

Autocracy is also connected with empire. Pipes writes: 'Russia has had to administer too vast a territory with too limited resources to indulge in democracy'.[68] In Putin's Russia this logic is illustrated by Chechnya. Chechnya undoubtedly strengthened the Russian security state. Putin claims the war has been won: there have been no suicide bombings in Moscow since 2004 and the level of local violence has sharply de-escalated, though at the cost of handing power in Grozny to a colourful and brutal gangster, Ramzan Kadyrov. According to the historian Geoffrey Hosking, the Russian empire (*Rossia*) has always prevented the political development of the Russian nation (*Rus*). Russia had to become a nation before it could become a democracy.[69] It seemed that this was about to happen when Russia pulled out of the USSR. It has now become clearer, as I have pointed out, that the end of the Soviet empire did not automatically spell the end of the imperial state.

A third explanation for the re-emergence of autocracy pays less attention to ancient history, and more to the dynamics of revolution. According to Vladimir Mau, the collapse of the old regime (in this case communism) weakens the state and fragments society to such an extent that support grows for the reimposition of order by force. Thus, the 'regime of personal dictatorship' arises from the ashes of revolution, whether it be that of Cromwell, Napoleon, or Stalin.[70] Whether the present Putin phase will be followed by a consolidation of the dictatorship or the growth of a competitive democracy depends on the choice between nation-state and empire.[71]

Conclusion

My interest has been in what happens when the pull of a country's history comes up against the constraints of its international position. Will the country try to weaken the constraints? Or will it adjust to them? The first may involve international conflict, the second domestic conflict. My own tentative conclusions are as follows:

1. The attempt to impose 'liberal empire' or 'sovereign democracy' on the seceded parts of the old Soviet Union will fail. Russia is bound to exercise a large influence on the former Soviet territories, but it will have to share that influence with others. Russian has too little to offer for exclusive dominance. The EU, the United States, and China offer the former Soviet republics opportunities for 'balancing' against Russia. On the other hand, the projects of Surkov and Chubais may be realized in voluntary form. It is not so difficult to envisage the voluntary reincorporation of the ethnic Russian populations of Belarus, western Ukraine and northern Kazakhstan into the Russian Federation – but only in a context in which Russia emerges as a true regional leader offering an alternative to the EU. Alternatively (or coincidentally) Russia might discover a new business centre of gravity in Central Asia and East Asia, though this would hardly be the 'liberal empire' Chubais envisaged: more like the mutual attraction of autocrats.

2. Russia will not transform its economic system into an Anglo-American type of economy. Apart from their incapacity to do so, Russians are perfectly well aware of the faults of the Anglo-American model. We may see some compromise between a European (Sarkozy-style) and authoritarian, protectionist capitalism with a lot of industrial policy. This the kind of civilizational choice that sovereign countries are entitled to make for themselves.

3. The territorial and economic imperatives of empire will continue to make it difficult for Russia to evolve a

political system which conforms to Western norms. The middle class will expand, but there is no assurance it will become 'liberal' in the Western sense. So the Russian political system will probably remain autocratic for the foreseeable future, with a facade of democracy. This is disappointing, but is nevertheless an improvement on anything it has experienced, except in the briefest moments, in the past.

4. It is hard to see Russia offering the world a new type of universalism, as it once did with communism. The Russian strain of political messianism is pretty much exhausted. Nevertheless, Russia may be able to develop, out of its own spiritual and cultural resources, an attractive alternative to both the American and European models, provided it achieves long run economic success.

If the attempt to make Russia into an independent centre of power to rival the USA (and eventually China) fails, what role will it then play? A suggestive analogy may be with France during the long period of Anglo-American hegemony. Broadly speaking, France has acted the role of 'awkward partner' in the Anglo-American club – something which has continued right up to its orchestration of opposition to the Iraq war in 2003. On two occasions in the 20th century France helped to bring down the world monetary system – in 1931 and again in 1969-70. De Gaulle took France out of the NATO military alliance in 1966. France, uniquely in western Europe, built its own independent nuclear deterrent, and has been a champion of creating a European military capacity outside NATO. Without explicitly challenging US leadership, France tried to build its own *Ostpolitik* with Russia; and to use its axis with Germany to create a European position on foreign policy. The French have been the most insistent that Europe has interests which are not identical to America's – particularly in the Middle East, where France has been pro-Arab. There is a parallel between Putin and De Gaulle – both leaders trying to rescue their countries from humilitation and defeat and carve out a role consonant with national feelings of mission and pride. Both leaders interpreted national interest as 'sovereignty'.

France's dream of creating an independent centre has never succeeded, but the role of 'awkward partner' has given a distinctive flavour to French diplomacy, and it may be equally viable for a shrunken, proud, but no longer hegemonic Russia. The analogy is not exact, since shared interests and values put a limit on France's truculence, which may be lacking in Russia's case. But a similar role may be viable for a shrunken, proud, but no longer hegemonic Russia – one which may offer Russia its best hope of reconciling its yearning for independence with the realities of the modern world.

Notes

1   I would like to thank Pavel Erochkine, Victor Masch, Louis Mosley, Andrew Tyrie and Shirley Williams for their helpful comments.

2   Jonathan Steele argues that the two countries' relations with each other are far warmer than either US-Russian or US-Chinese relations. 'The Sino-Russian Embrace leaves the US out in the

Cold', *Guardian*, 12 October 2007. Examples of a Russia-Asia axis are the Collective Security Treaty Organization, set up in 2003, which includes Russia, Armenia, Belarus, Kazakhstan, Kyrgyzstan, Tajikistan, and Uzbekistan. Then there is the Shanghai Cooperation Organization, started in 2001, which includes Russia and several Central Asian countries.

3 Roderic Lyne, Strobe Talbot and Koji Watanabe, 'Growing Pains or a Paradigm Shift? A Trilateral View of a Changing Relationship with Russia', *Russia in Global Affairs*, vol.4, no.4, October-December 2006, http://eng.globalaffairs.ru/numbers/17/1073.html.

4 'A long-term vision for Russian foreign policy may still be lacking'. Bobo Lo, *Vladimir Putin and the Evolution of Russian Foreign Policy*, (Blackwell, 2003) p. 4.

5 'The Foreign Policy Concept of the Russian Federation', 28 June 2000. Unofficial Translation. http://www.fas.org/nuke/guide/russia/doctrine/econcept.htm.

6 Unilateralism, Primakov thought, 'runs counter to objective processes in the world economy and international relations'. Yevgeny Primakov, 'A World without Superpowers', *Russia in Global Affairs*, vol.1, no.3, July-September 2003, http://eng.globalaffairs.ru/numbers/4/484.html.

7 President Putin's speech to the 43rd Munich Conference on Security Policy, 10 February 2007, http://www.securityconference.de/konferenzen/rede.php?sprache=en&id=179.

8 'Heated Words Have No Place in a Post-Cold War World', *Financial Times*, 1 May 2007.

9 Putin Speech, 10 February 2007, see fn. 6 above. See also 'Appendix: The World According to Surkov', *Heritage Foundation*, no. 1940, 1 June 2006, p. 9.

10 Russian attitudes to Gorbachev are still unforgiving. Far from seeing him as a purveyor of a humanistic universalism, most

Russians see him – most unfairly – as at best a bungler, at worst a traitor. I was once shown round the back of Lenin's mausoleum in Red Square, where there is a sequence of plinths on which are mounted busts of former Soviet leaders. There was an empty space after Chernenko. 'A place for Gorbachev?' I suggested to the Russian officer who accompanied me. 'No, his place is in Washington', he replied grimly.

11 Primakov, 'A World without Superpowers', see fn. 5 above.

12 Dominic Lieven, *Empire: The Russian Empire and Its Rivals* (John Murray, 2000), p. 66.

13 One could argue that Ireland was an exception in the British case, and Algeria in the French case. Both were part of the 'mother country', though they did not feel that way.

14 The phrase is Veronika Krasheninnikova's from her brilliant 'America-Russia: Cold War of Cultures', Synopsis, ("Europe" Publishing, 2007) p. 3.

15 Anatoly Chubais, 'Russia's Mission in the 21st Century', *Nezavisimaya Gazeta*, 1 October 2003. Reprinted in *Johnson's Russia List*, no. 7347, Article 4, 1 October 2003.

16 Cf. Alexander Prokhanov, editor-in-chief of *Zavtra*: 'Russia can't be a medieval geopolitical empire, it should be the empire of the XXI century, the type of power that the USA is currently exercising'. Quoted in 'United States of Russia to save the nation from final destruction', *Pravda*, 14 December 2004.

17 Vladislav Surkov's speeches: 'General'naya Liniya', *Moskovskie Novosti*, no. 7 (1234) March 3-9, 2006; 'General'naya Liniya', *Moskovskie Novosti*, no. 8 (1235) March 10-16, 2006; 'How Russia should fight international conspiracies', delivered to Delovaya Rossiya (Business Russia) Economic Forum, www.mosnews.com, 12 July 2005. See also Surkov's interview, 'The West doesn't have to love us', *Der Spiegel*, 20 June 2005.

18 'United States of Russia to save the nation from final destruction', *Pravda*, 14 December 2004.

19 Successful in 1914, until the Tsarist regime collapsed, as well as in 1812 and 1941.

20 A well-known interpretation of Anglo-Russian relations is that during the 19th century Britain tried to encircle Russian southern borders with an "Islamic belt" («исламский пояс»), a buffer of Muslim states. See Владимир Карпец, круглый стол «Лондон-Москва. Истоки кризиса», quoted on www.politjournal.ru, 29 October 2007.

21 Lieven, *Empire*, p. 205.

22 For Chubais quotations see fn. 13 above.

23 For Surkov quotations see fn. 15 above.

24 The Marquis de Custine, *Empire of the Czar: A Journey through Eternal Russia* (Doubleday, 1971) first published in 1843, p. 161.

25 Lieven, *Empire*, p. 220.

26 In April 2007, the Estonian government decided to remove the Soviet war memorial in the centre of Tallinn. An ethnic Russian died in protest riots. Russia retaliated by suspending rail traffic and other threats.

27 For a compendium of EU-Russia disagreements, and analysis of areas of potential co-operation see Katinka Barysch, 'Russia, realism and EU Unity', *Centre for European Reform Policy Brief*, July 2007.

28 Nazdezhada Arbatova and Vladimir Ryzhkov, 'Russia and the European Union: in Search of a Common Strategy', *Report of Russia in the United Europe*, 2006, p. 38.

29 Pavel K. Baev, 'Putin's European Project Derailed or setback in Reformatting?' *PONARS Policy Memo. no.331*, November 2004. For PONARS series see http://www.csis.org/ruseura/ponars/. See also Bobo Lo, *Vladimir Putin and the Evolution of Russian Foreign Policy*, ch. 4.

30 *Financial Times*, 8 November 2001.

31 *Financial Times*, 26 October 2001, and 22 November 2001.

32 Putin's failure to modernize Russia's armed forces is a serious setback for his attempt to project Russian power. What makes failure tolerable is the EU's inability to upgrade and expand their own military forces. This allows Putin to brag about missiles which can penetrate the West's air defence.

33 Quoted by Andrew Jack in the *Financial Times*, 12 November 2001, and *Financial Times*, 21 April 2006.

34 'The Next Shock?' *Economist*, 4 March 1999.

35 'Pipeline disputes and the hydrocarbon wealth now coming online in Central Asia have encouraged Russia to greatly increase the political significance attached to trade within the CIS'. Roland Nash, 'The Kremlin Shifts Gear in 2007', *Renaissance Capital Research*, 19 February 2007.

36 'Wolfgang Munchau: The EU needs a Joint Response', *Financial Times*, 8 May 2006.

37 *Financial Times*, 20 September 2007, *International Herald Tribune*, 21 September 2007. The Commission's strategy is not aimed solely at Gazprom. Under its proposals, big EU energy generating companies like EDF in France and Eon in Germany would also have to sell their transmission networks.

38 Lieven, *Empire*, p. xvi.

39 See 'Russia's Liberal Empire', *Asia Times Online*, 18 December 2003, http://www.atimes.com/atimes/Central_Asia/EL18Ag01.html.

40 'The logic of Putin's policy of centralization has created a Russian state with a centralized and semi-autocratic presidential regime, weakened federalism, a sham parliament, a subordinate judiciary, correuption even greater than in the 1990s, a weak and purposefully deformed party system, and limitations on democratic freedoms including the electronic mass media'. Irina Kobrinskaya,

'Russia–NIS Relations Beyond the Colour Revolutions: Are the Shifts Durable?', *PONARS Policy Memo. no.375*, December 2005.

41 'Managing the Retreat: Can Russia Adapt to the Emergence of Intermediate Europe?' *PONARS Policy Memo. no.391*, December 2005.

42 IMF, World Economic Outlook Database, October 2007, for the year 2006, http://www.imf.org/external/pubs/ft/weo/2007/02/weodata/index.aspx.

43 Human Development Report 2006, compiled on the basis of 2004 data, http://hdr.undp.org/en/statistics/.

44 Article 4: 'In order to ensure security and maintain peace and stability, the sides… grant each other the right to use military facilities on their territory.' http://www.kremlin.ru.

45 Robert Skidelsky and Pavel Erochkine, "Unilateral Visa Disarmament Can Save Russia", *Moscow Times*, 28 May 2003. Cf. Craig Mellow, 'Red Star Rising', *Institutional Investor*, February 2007, p. 68, on the 'devilish visa procedures' which impede tourism.

46 Nazdezhada Arbatova and Vladimir Ryzhkov, 'Russia and the European Union: in Search of a Common Strategy', p. 42. See also Fiona Hill, 'Energy Empire: Oil, Gas and Russia's Revival', *Foreign Policy Centre*, September 2004.

47 Michael Byers, *War Law: Understanding International Law and Conflict* (Atlantic Books, 2005), p. 10.

48 Deepak Lal, *In Praise of Empires: Globalization and Order* (Palgrave Macmillan, 2004), p. 72.

49 Edward Luttwak, 'Dead End: Counterinsurgency warfare as military malpractice', *Harpers Magazine*, February 2007. For a contrary view, which emphasises US military power, see Alexander Goltz, 'Warfare against the Rules', *Russia in Global Affairs*, vol.1, no.3, July-September 2003, http://www.eng.globalaffairs.ru/numbers/4/486.html.

50 'The Correlates of War', http://www.correlatesofwar.org/. See also Bennett, D. Scott, and Allan Stam, 2000. 'Eugene: A Conceptual Manual', *International Interactions*, 26, pp. 179-204, http://eugenesoftwar.org.

51 Data from the Economist Intelligence Unit Database.

52 Vladimir Shlapentokh, 'Russia's Demographic Decline and the Public Reaction', *Europe-Asia Studies*, vol.57, No.7,November 2005, pp. 951-2.

53 Ibid., p. 964.

54 Dmitry Gorenberg,'The 2002 Russian Census and the Future of the Russian Population', *PONARS Policy Memo. no.319*, November 2003.

55 Yuri Krupnov and Ilnur Batyrshin, 'Space Industry Cluster in Russia's Amur Region', *EIR*, 28 September 2007.

56 There are ambitious plans afoot to make 'the Far East a comfortable and attractive place for people to live', Vladimir Putin, Speech to the State Council of the Russian Federation, 20 December 2006. Quoted in Yuri Krupnov and Ilnur Batyrshin, 'Space Industry Cluster in Russia's Amur Region', p. 48.

57 IMF, World Economic Outlook Database, October 2007, for the year 2006, http://www.imf.org/external/pubs/ft/weo/2007/02/weodata/index.aspx.

58 Energy Information Administration, official Energy Statistics from the US Government, http://www.eia.doe.gov/

59 Russia does not have market power in oil, though it does in gas. Russia has hedged against the possibility of a collapse in the oil price by setting up an Oil Stabilization Fund, which has accumulated $100 billion to ease any required fiscal adjustment.

60 But Western business leaders welcome the stability which the Putin system provides. See Nick Cohen, 'Look who's getting into bed with Vladimir', *Observer*, 4 October 2007.

61 Tony Wood points out that most of the post-Soviet investment has been directed to repairing existing capacity rather than towards diversifying the economy. '[This] suggests that the Russian business elite remains largely extractive in nature. Unless and until this orientation changes, GDP growth will continue to depend above all on the vagaries of global oil prices'. Tony Wood, 'Contours of the Putin Era: a Response to Vladimir Popov', *New Left Review*, 44, March-April 2007, http://www.newleftreview.org/?view=2659. See also Vladimir and Pavel Erochkine, *Russia's Oil Industry: Current Problems and Future Trends* (Centre for Global Studies, 2006), esp. chapters 5-7.

62 Because policy failures can be kept secret. See Georgy Egorov, Sergei Guriev and Konstantin Sonin, 'Media Freedom, Bureaucratic Incentives, and the Resource Curse', *Mimeo*, February 2007.

63 According to Vladimir Popov, the victory of 'Yedinstvo, the "party of power" in the 1999 legislative elections, was among other things, a victory for the have-nots (subsidized regions) over the haves (donor regions)'. This enabled Putin to centralize the government by appointing presidential viceroys, reforming the Federation Council, and changing the fiscal distribution formula. Vladimir Popov, 'Russia Redux?', *New Left Review*, 44, March-April 2007, http://www.newleftreview.org/?view=2658.

64 Richard Pipes, *A Concise History of the Russian Revolution* (Knopf, 1995), *Property and Freedom* (Knopf, 1999).

65 Richard Pipes, 'Flight from Freedom', *Moscow Times*, 9 August 2004.

66 Alexander Lukin, 'Pipes can't see the Trees for the Forest', *Moscow Times*, 21 July 2004.

67 Lieven, *Empire*, p. 251.

68 Pipes, 'Flight from Freedom', *Moscow Times*, 9 August 2004.

69 For the most succinct statement of this thesis see Geoffrey Hosking, *Russia: People and Empire, 1552-1917* (HarperCollins, 1997).

70 Vladimir Mau and Irina Starodubrovoskaya, *The Challenge of Revolution: Contemporary Russia in Historical Perspective* (Oxford, 2001).

71 For an optimistic prognostication, based on the results of the fourteen regional legislative elections held on 11 March 2007, see 'Political Competition on the up', *Trusted Sources*, 16 March 2007. For a more pessimistic assessment see '2007-2008 parliamentary and presidential elections', *Equity Research, Renaissance Capital*, 23 April 2007.